DREAM JOBS IN
ARCHITECTURE
AND
CONSTRUCTION

ADRIANNA MORGANELLI

W9-AKD-161
3 4028 09377 5568
HARRIS COUNTY PUBLIC LIBRARY

DISCARD

CRABTREE
PUBLISHING COMPANY
WWW.CRABTREEBOOKS.COM

CUTTING-EDGE CAREERS IN
TECHNICAL EDUCATION

Author:
Adrianna Morganelli

Series research and development:
Reagan Miller

Editorial director:
Kathy Middleton

Editor:
Petrice Custance

Proofreader:
Lorna Notsch

Design, photo research, and prepress:
Katherine Berti

Print and production coordinator:
Katherine Berti

Photographs:
iStockphoto
   BartCo: p. 27 (left)
   sturti: p. 29
NASA
   Tony Gray: p. 5 (bottom left)
Shutterstock
   attilavalentina: p. 12 (top)
   Claudio Stocco: p. 22 (bottom left)
   Featureflash Photo Agency: p. 5 (top)
   Gubin Yury: p. 23 (center right)
   J. Lekavicius: p. 5 (bottom right)
   Kathy Hutchins: p. 4 (bottom)
   Sean Pavone: p. 9 (right)
   shufu photoexperience: p. 15 (bottom right)
   vivooo: p. 13 (bottom)
   wangbin6007: p. 8
   Zoran Karapancev: p. 16–17 (bottom)
All other images by Shutterstock

Library and Archives Canada Cataloguing in Publication

Morganelli, Adrianna, 1979-, author
     Dream jobs in architecture & construction / Adrianna Morganelli.
(Cutting-edge careers in technical education)
Includes index.
Issued in print and electronic formats.
ISBN 978-0-7787-4437-5 (hardcover).--
ISBN 978-0-7787-4448-1 (softcover).--
ISBN 978-1-4271-2028-1 (HTML)
     1. Architecture--Vocational guidance--Juvenile literature. 2. Architects--
Training of--Juvenile literature. 3. Construction industry--Vocational
guidance--Juvenile literature. 4. Construction industry--Employees--Training
of-- Juvenile literature. I. Title.
NA1995.M67 2018   j720.23   C2018-900255-7
                                          C2018-900256-5

Library of Congress Cataloging-in-Publication Data

Names: Morganelli, Adrianna, 1979- author.
Title: Dream jobs in architecture & construction / Adrianna Morganelli.
Other titles: Dream jobs in architecture and construction
Description: New York, N.Y. : Crabtree Publishing Company, [2018] |
   Series: Cutting-edge careers in technical education | Includes index.
Identifiers: LCCN 2018004032 (print) | LCCN 2018006057 (ebook) |
   ISBN 9781427120281 (Electronic) |
   ISBN 9780778744375 (hardcover : alk. paper) |
   ISBN 9780778744481 (pbk. : alk. paper)
Subjects: LCSH: Building--Vocational guidance--Juvenile literature. |
   Architecture--Vocational guidance--Juvenile literature.
Classification: LCC TH159 (ebook) | LCC TH159 .M68 2018 (print) |
   DDC 690.023--dc23
LC record available at https://lccn.loc.gov/2018004032

Crabtree Publishing Company

www.crabtreebooks.com   1-800-387-7650

Printed in the U.S.A./052018/CG20180309

Copyright © 2018 CRABTREE PUBLISHING COMPANY. All rights reserved. No part of this publication may be reproduced, stored in a retrieval system or be transmitted in any form or by any means, electronic, mechanical, photocopying, recording, or otherwise, without the prior written permission of Crabtree Publishing Company. In Canada: We acknowledge the financial support of the Government of Canada through the Canada Book Fund for our publishing activities.

Published in Canada
Crabtree Publishing
616 Welland Ave.
St. Catharines, Ontario
L2M 5V6

Published in the United States
Crabtree Publishing
PMB 59051
350 Fifth Avenue, 59th Floor
New York, New York 10118

Published in the United Kingdom
Crabtree Publishing
Maritime House
Basin Road North, Hove
BN41 1WR

Published in Australia
Crabtree Publishing
3 Charles Street
Coburg North
VIC 3058

CONTENTS

INTRODUCTION TO CTE

Do you love a challenge? Do you enjoy working with your hands or figuring out how things work? How about designing a stunning gown or the best online game ever? If you said yes, Career and Technical Education is the key to landing your dream job.

Career and Technical Education (CTE) programs combine academic studies, such as math and science, with valuable hands-on training. CTE students develop job-specific skills that are in high demand by employers. CTE programs are divided into 16 career clusters. Some examples of these career clusters are Information Technology (IT), Human Services, Arts and Communications, Manufacturing, and Hospitality and Tourism. Each CTE career cluster is divided into job pathways. Each job pathway is a grouping of jobs that require similar interests and paths of study. For example, in the Manufacturing cluster, the Programming and **Software** Development pathway includes jobs such as game developer and software design engineer.

DID YOU KNOW?

Not enough young people are considering jobs in the CTE industry. As a result, there is a shortage of skilled workers in many industries. CTE jobs will always be in demand, since they are necessary for making, maintaining, and operating almost everything. CTE jobs pay high wages, and it costs students far less money and time to receive training and the necessary skills to do these jobs.

With the 2018 movie *A Wrinkle in Time*, Ava DuVernay became the first African American woman to direct a big-budget live-action film. Many other CTE professionals were involved in the making of this movie, including the camera operators, film editors, special effects teams, lighting and sound engineers, hair and makeup artists, and costume designers.

A

WHY CTE?

By 2020, around 10 million new skilled workers will be needed in the United States alone. This huge demand means there are many great opportunities out there for you! There is a wide variety of exciting CTE careers. If you're not quite sure which direction you want to head in yet, there are many online quizzes or activities that can help you discover your interests. But you don't have to choose a career right now. This is your time to explore!

Employers need people who embrace challenge. Whether discovering a new way to cook fish or figuring out how to launch a new rocket, if you can look at problems in new or different ways, then you are an ideal CTE candidate.

APPRENTICESHIPS

Within CTE industries, students have the opportunity to become **apprentices**, learning the skills of a profession while earning a paycheck to do it. Apprenticeships are available in many industries, including construction, health care, and manufacturing, and depending on the field, last several years. Trade professionals train the students in the classroom, as well as on actual jobs, so students are able to practice their skills in the real world.

Diane Sawyer has been a respected broadcast journalist for more than 50 years. She has interviewed some of the most **influential** people in the world.

On February 6, 2018, SpaceX, the American **aerospace** manufacturing company run by Elon Musk, launched its Falcon Heavy rocket. Attached to the rocket was a Tesla roadster with Starman, a mannequin in a spacesuit, at the wheel. The roadster is now cruising through space. You can track its location at www.whereisroadster.com.

ARCHITECTURE
AND CONSTRUCTION

You are about to embark on an exciting journey of learning about the many different careers you can explore within the architecture and construction industry!

If you have ever dreamed of designing, planning, managing, building, or maintaining the structures that people use to live, work, and play, then a career in the architecture and construction industry is for you. Have you ever pictured yourself designing skyscrapers? Then maybe being an architect is in your future. Have you ever wondered what it would be like to plow through the ground with a bulldozer? Perhaps a job as a heavy equipment operator is right for you.

SkillsUSA and Skills Canada promote CTE programs in schools. Both organizations offer competitions for students across all CTE career clusters at both the state/provincial and national levels.

ARCHITECTURE AND CONSTRUCTION JOB PATHWAYS:

DESIGN AND PRE-CONSTRUCTION	People in these careers turn a concept into a set of plans that guide construction professionals in the building process.
CONSTRUCTION	These jobs involve building everything from houses to chemical plants and highways.
MAINTENANCE AND OPERATIONS	People in these jobs ensure that establishments operate safely and efficiently. Some jobs include installing machinery.

HOW TO USE THIS BOOK

Each two-page spread focuses on a specific career in the Architecture and Construction CTE cluster. For each career, you will find a detailed description of life on the job, advice on the best educational path to take (see right), and tips on what you can do now to begin preparing for your dream job.

Electricians must pass a color test! The only way to tell the difference between multiple types of wires is a color-coded system, so excellent color vision is a necessity.

YOUR PATH

SECONDARY SCHOOL

This section lists the best subjects to take in high school.

POST-SECONDARY

Some jobs require an apprenticeship and **certification** while others require a college or university degree. This section gives you an idea of the best path to take after high school.

DID YOU KNOW?

In 2006, Marissa McTasney from Whitby, Canada, founded Moxie Trades, which began as a company that employed teams of women to do home renovations. As a woman who worked in construction, Marissa wanted to wear pink work boots. When she couldn't find any, she decided to evolve Moxie Trades into a safety equipment company featuring safety boots for women. Marissa named her company Moxie Trades because moxie means "courage and determination," which she feels are important for women working in CTE careers.

In the United States in 2016, there were more than 6.5 million people working in construction. By 2026, that number is expected to grow to more than 7.5 million.

ARCHITECT

Have you ever dreamed of designing a skyscraper or a beautiful mansion? Imagine the pride you would feel as an architect, when after all your hard work, you see your design finally built!

Architects create designs for buildings such as houses, shopping centers, and hospitals. Nearly every building in the world begins with an architect's design. Architects' finished designs are on **blueprints** that other construction professionals use to create a plan for building. Not only do architects consider a building's physical appearance, they also have to make sure it is economical, safe, and functional.

ON THE JOB

Architects lead the development of projects from early ideas to the final designs. This includes studying how a new building will affect existing buildings nearby, as well as the building site itself. There may be **structural** problems that the architect will need to find practical solutions for. Architects must also file **permit** applications with building departments and figure out how much their project will cost. They also visit the site during construction to check that the building is going according to plan.

Not only do architects design homes, they also design enormous structures such as hotels, university buildings, and skyscrapers.

WHAT CAN YOU DO NOW?

Learn how different structures are built, such as skyscrapers. Search online for tutorials or computer-generated models that show the stages of building. Ask a family member or trusted adult to take you on a tour of local buildings. Write down what you think is interesting about each building's design. Join a young architects' club or start your own.

DID YOU KNOW?

Frank Lloyd Wright is one of the most famous American architects in the world. Over a career that spanned 70 years, Wright designed more than 1,000 structures, and 532 of them were completed. His designs were based on his philosophy that structures should be designed in **harmony** with their natural surroundings.

YOUR PATH TO WORK AS AN ARCHITECT

SECONDARY SCHOOL

Math, physics, chemistry, art, economics, and CTE architecture courses are a great start.

POST-SECONDARY

A college or university degree is required.

Frank Lloyd Wright's most famous design work is Fallingwater, a house built partly over a waterfall in Pennsylvania.

Architectural models allow architects to test their designs and troubleshoot any structural problems before building.

CAD TECHNICIAN

CAD technicians use technology to design all types of buildings, from small houses to enormous **industrial** buildings, as well as machinery.

Computer-aided design (CAD) technicians convert verbal and written plans into electronic drawings. They create **3-D** representations of a design that engineers can take a **virtual** tour of. Their designs are created using special software programs, and they specify the **dimensions** of buildings or pieces of machinery, as well as what materials are needed to build them.

Computer-aided design is used to create photo **simulations**. Technicians **superimpose** designs of buildings that haven't been built yet on top of photographs of existing environments to determine what a site will look like.

Engineers review an electronic drawing of a design for a new shopping mall. They can inspect the design for potential structural problems and fix them before building begins.

YOUR PATH TO WORK AS A CAD TECHNICIAN

SECONDARY SCHOOL

Focus on math, science, computers, physics, chemistry, and economics courses.

POST-SECONDARY

A CAD college program or university degree in architectural design is required.

DID YOU KNOW?

CAD technicians are employed in several different industries, including construction, manufacturing, engineering, government, communications, and broadcasting.

ON THE JOB

Your ability to work as a part of a team is an important skill that you should have as a CAD technician. You will be required to collaborate with a team of engineers and other technicians to develop a particular design. Usually, each member is assigned a separate area of a project, but all of the areas must build upon each other. CAD technicians must stay up-to-date on the new versions of software they are using. They must be able to evolve, or grow, along with their advancing computer programs.

WHAT CAN YOU DO NOW?

Learn all you can about CAD. Search online for tutorials or free demonstrations for creating 3-D representations and give it a try. Join a computer design club or start your own. See if there are any CTE groups in your area offering activities or summer camps with a computer-design element.

CAD technicians create electronic versions of technical drawings created by **drafters**.

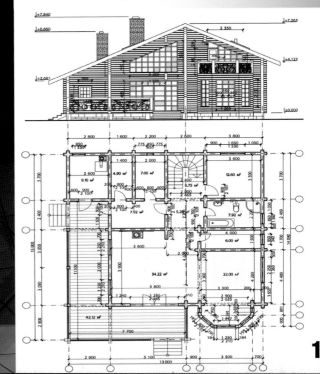

BRICKLAYER

As long as humans continue to need shelter, bricklaying will be a profession that will always be high in demand.

ON THE JOB

If you are creative and like to work with your hands, a career in bricklaying may be right for you. Bricklayers lay bricks, stone, concrete blocks, and other materials to build and repair structures, including houses and chimneys. They may also line furnaces and fireplaces with firebrick, which is brick that can withstand intense heat. Bricklayers create **installations** based on blueprints and sketches. Some of their work may involve **intricate** designs, so it is helpful that they have a flair for composition, color, and **proportion**. Bricklayers are required to cut and trim bricks and other materials, so bricklayers must know how to use hand and power tools.

The Dr Chau Chak Wing Building in Sydney, Australia, was designed by Frank Gehry, a Canadian-born American architect. It is estimated that 320,000 custom-made bricks were used in its construction.

Bricklaying is one of the world's oldest professions. Mohenjo-daro in Pakistan is the site of one of the world's oldest cities. The buildings were made of **mortared brick** and **mud-brick** that had been dried in the Sun.

YOUR PATH TO WORK AS A BRICKLAYER

SECONDARY SCHOOL

Focus on math, statistics, science, and CTE construction courses.

POST-SECONDARY

On-the-job training and apprenticeships are available.

WHAT CAN YOU DO NOW?

Learn about the different methods of laying brick. Ask for permission to build a small walled garden in your backyard. Search online for tutorials and instructions to guide you. Carefully draw up plans for your walled garden before you begin building. Can you spot any potential problems with your design? Troubleshoot your plans and then start building!

DID YOU KNOW?

Whoopi Goldberg, the American actress, used to be a bricklayer!

Bricklayers are trained to do their jobs safely. They wear protective hard hats and use safety harnesses and **scaffolding**.

CARPENTER

In the past, carpenters only worked with natural wood. Today, they build all sorts of structures with many different building materials, including **engineered lumber**.

Do you get satisfaction from making things? Are you precise when you work, and pay close attention to detail? If so, you may consider venturing into carpentry. Not only do carpenters need good math skills, they also need imagination as their job requires them to create every day.

There are many different types of carpentry jobs. For example, finish carpentry is an artistic job for which exact **joints** are important to create fine woodworking, such as cabinetry, furniture, models, and instruments.

ON THE JOB

As a carpenter, you will build, install, and repair structures that are made of wood and other materials. The duties of a carpenter are endless! One day you may install floor beams, walls, and roofs to buildings, and the next you may build and install wood finishes inside homes, such as trim and baseboards, staircases, and **molding**. Carpenters also repair wooden structures that have been damaged or have become unsafe or unstable. You will need to measure on your job, lift heavy materials, and cut wood with hand and power tools before you fit pieces together. To do your job accurately, you will need to learn how to read blueprints and drawings and to make quick mental calculations.

WHAT CAN YOU DO NOW?

Research different forms of woodworking. Search online for tutorials and building projects that you can try. Remember to get an adult's permission before you begin a project! Join a woodworking or young carpenters' club or start your own club at your school.

YOUR PATH TO WORK AS A CARPENTER

SECONDARY SCHOOL

Math, statistics, language arts, biology, physics, chemistry, and CTE woodworking classes are an excellent start.

POST-SECONDARY

A college diploma, apprenticeship, and certification are required.

DID YOU KNOW?

More than one-fourth of carpenters are self-employed.

Carpenters must be comfortable with heights.

A ship's carpenter specializes in shipbuilding.

CONCRETE FINISHER

Today, concrete is the most used human-made material in the world, and many jobs in the construction industry work with concrete, including concrete finishers.

If you are physically fit and enjoy working with tools and equipment, concrete finishing may be the job for you. Concrete finishers need to pay attention to detail and work efficiently, because working with concrete is time-sensitive. Once the ingredients to make concrete are mixed together, concrete finishers must put the concrete in place before it sets, or hardens.

ON THE JOB

As a concrete finisher, you will work with concrete being released directly from the chute of a concrete wagon, a pump, or a wheelbarrow. You will direct where the concrete is to go, and prepare concrete **forms**. It is very important that concrete finishers set the forms with the correct depth and **pitch**. Once it is poured, you will spread the concrete with shovels and rakes, and smooth or level it with trowels. You will then add a hardening sealer to the concrete, which speeds up the drying time and makes the concrete waterproof. Concrete finishers also repair and restore concrete that has already been set.

Concrete finishers **immerse** a tool called a concrete vibrator into the wet concrete to settle it into place within the form.

More than 21 million cubic yards (16 million cubic meters) of concrete were used to build the Three Gorges Dam in Hubei Province in China. This is the world record for the largest concrete pour.

WHAT CAN YOU DO NOW?

Learn about the different ways concrete is mixed. Search online for concrete-finishing tutorials to expand your knowledge. If a family member or other trusted adult is planning a do-it-yourself home project that involves pouring concrete, ask if you can help. Or maybe a professional concrete-pouring job is happening in your neighborhood. Ask for permission to go and watch the concrete finishers as they work.

YOUR PATH TO WORK AS A CONCRETE FINISHER

SECONDARY SCHOOL

Focus on math, statistics, science, and CTE construction courses.

POST-SECONDARY

On-the-job training and apprenticeships are available.

When the concrete is still wet, concrete finishers apply different finishes to the surface. Broom finishes are used to prevent people from slipping when they walk on the surface. A stamp finish comes in a variety of styles, and is used to make driveways, walkways, and patios unique.

CONSTRUCTION INSPECTOR

Making sure buildings are safe to use is the important job of a construction inspector. Without this job, every person's safety would be at risk!

Construction inspectors examine, or inspect, the safety of buildings based on the standards of a building code. Building codes are sets of rules that buildings must conform to in order to pass inspections. Construction inspectors enforce these codes for newly built structures and during remodeling projects. These buildings may be houses or commercial structures, such as stores and restaurants. Because building codes are always being updated, construction inspectors must stay current with any changes.

DID YOU KNOW?

Construction inspectors are employed by the government, as their job is to uphold the building codes of the regions in which they work.

When they are not in the office reviewing plans, construction inspectors are outside working on construction sites to perform their inspections.

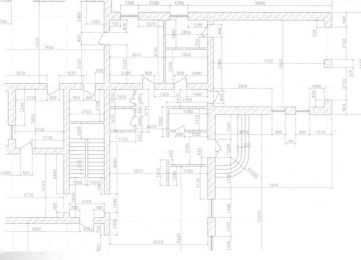

Construction inspectors must be able to read a building site's blueprints so they can properly inspect the site.

YOUR PATH TO WORK AS A CONSTRUCTION INSPECTOR

SECONDARY SCHOOL

Math, statistics, language arts, science, and CTE construction courses are a great start.

POST-SECONDARY

A college diploma in construction, civil engineering, or architectural technology, plus several years of related work experience, is required.

ON THE JOB

If you decide to work as a construction inspector, you will review the plans, drawings, and site layouts for buildings and issue building permits. You will be required to travel to worksites to conduct inspections on buildings to ensure they comply with the building code. Construction inspectors also inspect and test electrical and plumbing installations, as well as concrete forms and steel frameworks. After your inspection is complete, you will spend time writing technical reports of your findings.

WHAT CAN YOU DO NOW?

Learn all you can about construction practices. Research different styles of blueprints and study how to read them. Search online for tutorials and videos about different construction jobs to expand your knowledge.

Some of the tools construction inspectors use at a site are: an **infrared** thermometer, to spot temperature variations that may indicate insufficient insulation; a moisture meter, to spot leakage; and a multigas detector, to indicate if there are any dangerous gas leaks.

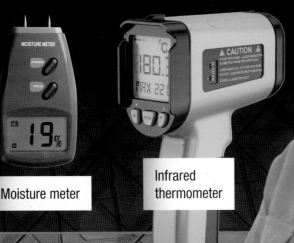

Moisture meter

Infrared thermometer

Multigas detector

ELECTRICIAN

The modern industrial world is powered by electricity, and electricians work to ensure that electrical power reaches people all over the world for a growing number of uses.

As an electrician, you will be a specialist in the electrical wiring of buildings, machinery, and equipment. Some electricians work with the wiring of airplanes, ships, and mobile systems, including phones, tablet computers, and handheld game **consoles**. If you decide to become an electrician, your job will be to assemble, install, and repair electrical wiring, equipment, and fixtures in all types of buildings and structures. Electricians troubleshoot electronic systems, as well as conduct programs that help keep these systems running effectively.

This electrician is testing electrical **circuits** on a power board.

ON THE JOB

The various duties of electricians take them to many different locations for work. As an electrician, you may be required to repair a circuit **breaker** inside a power plant on one day. On another day, your job may take you outside to install a lighting system on the exterior of a building. Electricians are hired by **contractors** and maintenance departments, and some electricians are self-employed.

WHAT CAN YOU DO NOW?

Learn all you can about electricity. Join an electronics club or start one of your own. If there is a hydroelectric power plant in your area, ask your teacher if your class can attend a tour there.

DID YOU KNOW?

The biggest blackout in North American history happened in 2003. A high-voltage power line in northern Ohio brushed against some overgrown trees. The line shut down, which then caused more lines to shut down. Fifty million people in Canada and the U.S. were without power for two days.

YOUR PATH TO WORK AS AN ELECTRICIAN

SECONDARY SCHOOL

Math, statistics, language arts, physics, chemistry, and CTE electronics classes are an excellent start.

POST-SECONDARY

A college program and certification are required.

Electricians often have to work up high when installing lights. Hard hats, harnesses, and sturdy scaffolding are important pieces of safety equipment.

Many schools have electronics labs. These labs provide a safe space for students to experiment and learn how electronics work.

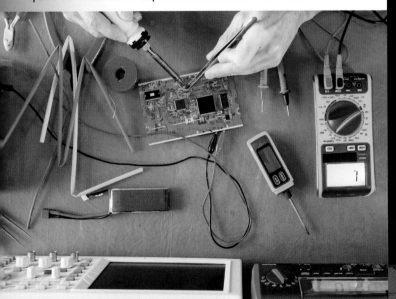

HEAVY EQUIPMENT
OPERATOR

Without heavy equipment, or heavy-duty vehicles, much of the work in the construction field would be more time-consuming and nearly impossible to complete!

Sometimes heavy equipment operators soar high into the sky, such as this crane operator working on top of a skyscraper.

Have you ever wondered what it would be like to handle some of the biggest and most powerful machines ever built? If so, heavy equipment operator may be just the career for you. Heavy equipment operators are skilled workers who operate vehicles that do jobs on construction sites that cannot be done by hand. They must have good judgment and be able to listen to and follow instructions, because they are responsible for machinery that could be dangerous if not handled properly.

ON THE JOB

There are different types of heavy equipment operators. Operating engineers use bulldozers, which clear and level land, and backhoes, which scoop and dump materials, dig trenches, and break concrete and rock. They also operate graders, which use blades to spread and level earth, and front-end loaders that pick up materials such as sand, gravel, and rock and dump them where needed. As a pile driver operator, you will be controlling machines that hammer heavy beams into the ground to support structures such as **retaining walls**, bridges, and building foundations. In addition to controlling heavy equipment, your job will also include cleaning and inspecting the machinery to ensure it is in good working condition.

Heavy equipment operators must work well with others. They work closely with other equipment operators and ground crew.

YOUR PATH TO WORK AS A HEAVY EQUIPMENT OPERATOR

SECONDARY SCHOOL

Focus on math, statistics, science, and CTE cconstruction courses.

POST-SECONDARY

On-the-job training and certification are available.

WHAT CAN YOU DO NOW?

Research and study different heavy equipment vehicles. Search online for videos and tutorials to learn how they operate. When you pass by a construction site, notice the vehicles in action. Sometimes heavy equipment is on display at fairs and festivals, and you can have a chance to explore and even sit inside.

When paving roadways, operators spread cement and asphalt with paving, surfacing, and **tamping** equipment.

Excavator

Grader

Bulldozer

IRONWORKER

Ironworking is an exciting career because there are many different types of ironwork, each with its own challenges and necessary skills.

ON THE JOB

If you don't get queasy working at great heights, structural ironworking could be a possible career for you. Structural ironworkers build the metal frameworks of buildings based on engineered drawings. In addition to large buildings, they also work on bridges, towers, and stadiums. Reinforcing ironworkers place steel bars in concrete forms to strengthen concrete structures. **Ornamental** ironworkers install metal windows in the openings of buildings and erect the walls that cover the reinforced structure of a building. They use many types of materials, including steel, bronze, and aluminum, to make and install stairways, railings, and fences, among other items. Ornamental ironworkers bolt or **weld** these additions to structures.

DID YOU KNOW?

When Jamie McMillan began her career as an ironworker in 2002, she encountered many people, including coworkers and bosses, who doubted her abilities because she was a woman. But she didn't let their attitudes discourage her. Instead, she trained hard and proved her abilities. After a few years in the trade, McMillan founded a program that **mentors** hundreds of young women who are considering a career in the trades. She also visits high schools and trade events to speak about women working in CTE industries.

These CTE students are learning the basics of ironwork.

WHAT CAN YOU DO NOW?

Research metals and the different methods of ironwork. Search online for videos and tutorials to learn more about the different techniques.

Safety is an ironworker's best friend. Harnesses and hard hats are essential for workers high up on scaffolding during a job.

YOUR PATH TO WORK AS AN IRONWORKER

SECONDARY SCHOOL

Focus on math, science, and CTE construction classes.

POST-SECONDARY

A college program, apprenticeship, and certification are required.

Decorative ironwork adds beauty and unique style to structures.

Depending on the size of the structures involved, an ironworker may work on a particular project for a few months or for years.

PLUMBER

If you are looking for a career that offers plenty of variety, then look no further than the plumbing field!

Plumbers install and repair plumbing equipment, such as pipes and fixtures, used to distribute water to people and places. This equipment is also used to dispose of **wastewater** in homes and commercial and industrial buildings. Ask yourself whether you enjoy working with machines and with your hands. Are you disciplined and precise in your work? Are you comfortable communicating with other people? If so, plumbing may be the perfect job for you.

ON THE JOB

If you decide to become a plumber, you will be required to use tools to cut openings in walls and floors to fit pipes and pipe fittings. You will also use hand and power tools to cut and bend pipes, and join them using screws, bolts, clamps, and cement. Plumbers are also good at welding. In addition to installing equipment, you will need to test pipes for leaks and prepare cost **estimates** for customers.

Plumbers are in demand almost everywhere because every home and building depends on fresh water intake, as well as disposal of wastewater.

WHAT CAN YOU DO NOW?

Research how plumbing systems work. Watch online video tutorials to learn more. The next time a family member or trusted adult peforms a do-it-yourself plumbing job, ask if you can help.

Once plumbers complete their apprenticeships, they choose which industry sector to work in. Many small companies specialize in plumbing for residences, but larger companies work in industrial buildings and on construction sites.

YOUR PATH TO WORK AS A PLUMBER

SECONDARY SCHOOL

Math, science, and CTE construction classes are a great start.

POST-SECONDARY

College programs, apprenticeships, and certification are available.

American inventor Philip Haas received more than 30 **patents** for inventions in the plumbing field. His inventions helped improve the reliability of the modern toilet.

REFRIGERATION/
AIR CONDITIONING MECHANIC

Without refrigeration and air conditioning mechanics, our food would spoil in grocery stores, and we would be uncomfortable inside buildings and homes that are too warm.

Refrigeration mechanics and air conditioning mechanics install central air conditioning systems and refrigeration systems in homes, stores, and industrial buildings. They perform maintenance on these systems to ensure that they are running properly, and if they are not, make the necessary repairs. These mechanics also work with systems that combine heating, **ventilation**, and cooling.

Refrigeration and air conditioning mechanics experience much variety on the job, as every project is different.

ON THE JOB

To enjoy a career as a mechanic in refrigeration and air conditioning, you need to like working with machines. You will be measuring and cutting piping before welding the pipes together, and will have to use hand and power tools to do installations. Refrigeration and air conditioning mechanics are good problem-solvers. They must identify problems with the systems and figure out ways to repair the machines' parts. An important part of your job will be to test the refrigeration and air conditioning systems for leaks and other problems.

WHAT CAN YOU DO NOW?

Learn how refrigeration and air conditioning systems work. Search online for simple experiments or activities dealing with cooling that you can try. Join an electronics club.

DID YOU KNOW?

Many refrigeration and air conditioning mechanics are employed by construction companies, contractors, food wholesalers, and engineering firms.

YOUR PATH TO WORK AS A REFRIGERATION/ AIR CONDITIONING MECHANIC

SECONDARY SCHOOL

Math, statistics, chemistry, and CTE electronics classes are an excellent start.

POST-SECONDARY

On-the-job training and certification are available.

Mechanics may work indoors or outdoors, with a team of other mechanics and construction professionals, or by themselves.

LEARNING MORE

BOOKS

Cohn, Jessica. *On the Job in Construction.* Red Chair, 2016.

Kopp, Megan. *Maker Projects for Kids Who Love Designing Spaces.* Crabtree, 2017.

Owen, Ruth. *Building Green Places: Careers in Planning, Designing, and Building.* Crabtree, 2009.

WEBSITES

WWW.CAREEROUTLOOK.US/ ASSESSMENT/SHORT.SHTML	Career Outlook	Check how your personal interests relate to the world of work. Find out the minimum education and growth outlook for each job.
HTTPS://SKILLUSA.ORG	SkillsUSA	This site offers resources and information on competitions, conferences, and other activities.
WWW.KENT.AC.UK/CAREERS/ SK/CARDS5.HTML	Employability Skills Game	Match skill descriptions with the word that describes the skill.

GLOSSARY

3-D Short for three-dimensional. An object that appears to have length, depth, and width.

aerospace A branch of technology specializing in air and space flight

apprentice Someone who is learning a skilled trade from a professional

blueprints Detailed drawings or plans for a project

breaker An automatic device that stops the flow of current in an electric circuit

certification Certificate that shows someone has achieved a certain level of skill and knowledge

circuit A complete path that an electric current flows around

console A panel of switches used to control an electrical device

contractor A person or company that agrees to provide materials or perform work

dimensions The length, area, and volume of an object

draft To draw sketches or plans

engineered lumber Bits of lumber that are formed together using heat or glue

estimate A judgment of how much something will cost

form A mold in which something is shaped

harmony An orderly or pleasing arrangement

immerse To plunge into something that surrounds

industrial Used in the manufacturing of goods

influential Someone whose opinion is taken seriously by others

infrared Able to be photographed in the dark

installation Something that has been built or put into place for use

intricate Highly complicated or detailed

joint The point at which parts of a structure are joined

mentor An experienced and trusted advisor

molding A decorative surface

mortared brick Bricks bound together with paste, usually made of cement

mud-brick Bricks made of mud, often dried in sunshine

ornamental Decorative or attractive in appearance

patent A license giving sole rights of an invention to the inventor

permit Legal written permission

pitch The steepness of a slope

proportion The correct relationship between size, shape, and position of the different parts of something

retaining wall A wall that is built to keep the land behind it from sliding

scaffolding A temporary structure used by workers to climb or stand on

simulation To imitate the operation of a process or system

software The programs and other operating information used by a computer

structural The part of a building's frame that holds its weight

superimpose To place or lay something over another thing

tamping To firmly pack down a substance

trowel A small tool for spreading plaster

ventilation Adding fresh air to a room or building

virtual Simulated on a computer

wastewater Water that has been used in a home or as part of an industrial process

weld To join pieces of metal together by heating and melting

County Public Library
Houston, Texas

INDEX